YOUR KNOWLEDGE HAS VALUE

Hemant Kumar Saini, Nitesh Chouhan

Detecting Veracity

A New door to keep Safe from fake Posts

GRIN Publishing

Bibliographic information published by the German National Library:

The German National Library lists this publication in the National Bibliography;
detailed bibliographic data are available on the Internet at http://dnb.dnb.de .

Imprint:

Copyright © 2014 GRIN Verlag GmbH
Print and binding: Books on Demand GmbH, Norderstedt Germany
ISBN: 978-3-656-85193-6

This book at GRIN:

http://www.grin.com/en/e-book/285280/detecting-veracity

GRIN - Your knowledge has value

Since its foundation in 1998, GRIN has specialized in publishing academic texts by students, college teachers and other academics as e-book and printed book. The website www.grin.com is an ideal platform for presenting term papers, final papers, scientific essays, dissertations and specialist books.

Detecting Veracity

A New door to keep Safe from fake Posts

Hemant Kumar Saini
M.Tech, Department of Computer Science & Engineering, RTU, Kota

&

Nitesh Chouhan
Assistant Professor, Department of Information Technology, MLV Government Textile & Engineering College, Bhilwara (Rajasthan).

Table of Contents

SR.No.   Page

1. Introduction   4

2. Identification   4

3. Classification of Information   5

4. Architecture   6

5. Detection   7

6. Conclusion   8

7. References   9

Foreword

 Mr. Hemant Kumar Saini is a Red hat Certified Engineer. He has obtained his M.Tech degree in Computer Science & Engineering in 2014.He has completed B.Tech from MLV Govt. Textile & Engineering College in 2011. He is the author of several articles published in reputed Journals and international Conferences.

E-mail: hemantrhce@rediffmail.com

 **Mr. NITESH CHOUHAN** is Assistant Professor in MLV Government Textile & Engineering College, Bhilwara (Rajasthan). He has completed M.E. and B.E. in Computer Science & Engineering. He is having 9 years of academic experience. His research interests are Software Testing and Cyber Security.

3

1. Introduction

In the present era of the distributed system where almost the complete world has been engaged in social networking, how one can claim that he/she get the real authenticated content. Since the content on the internet is not verified especially the social media content where the people post mostly the doubtful information. The main difficult problem is the filtering of truth from such contents. In such a situation social media find the new challenge of establishing veracity (doubtable data). So a new system PHEME is going to establish for analyzing the content in social sites, blogs and socially related posts based on the language and determine the uncertainty or the doubts in the content. This system will help not only in medical information systems (where causes serious damages if the wrong information held) but also in digital journalism.

The system is under developing phase which claims to check the posts on social networks like Facebook and Twitter and then only permit to publish on Webpage. The project is running by International Group of Researches under the University of Sheffield as part of GATE, the University of Warwick, and King's College London, Saarland University in Germany and MODUL University Vienna.

2. Identification

Pheme is deployed with combination of the various techniques such as NLP, Data Mining, Web, Social Networking and Information visualization. With these techniques combine together it analyzes the realism and identify the information as shown in Fig.1. The various steps involved in it are discussed as follows:

4

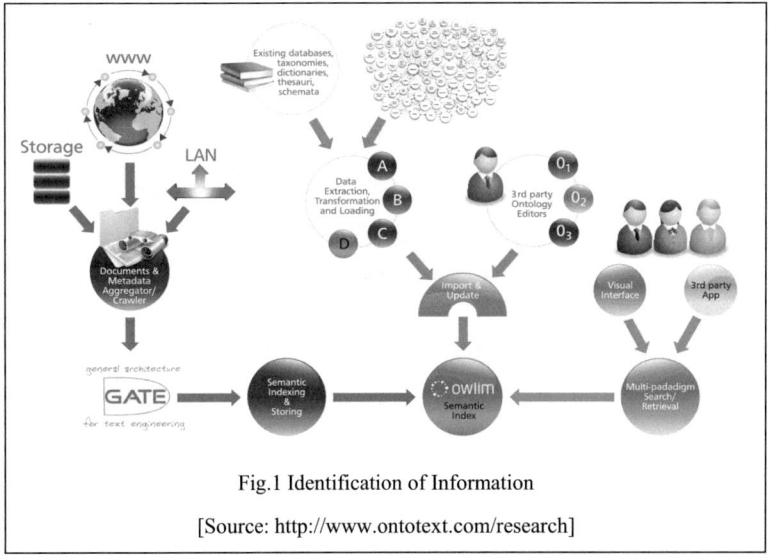

Fig.1 Identification of Information

[Source: http://www.ontotext.com/research]

- Firstly the lexical, semantic and syntactic information are collected from the data or the posts.

- Then the above collection is cross referenced with the Linked Open Data (LOD) through the expertise of Ontotext and various data sources using OWLIM platform.

- Next using the intelligent algorithms built in Sheffield's GATE text mining platform information is analyzed and detect it's reality.

- Following that it will spin out results in a visual interactive mode with the different categories which are discussed in next section.

3. Classification of information

The fake information on the social network based on the semantics and language context can be classified into four categories:

- Speculation – unverified statements

- Controversial- disputed messages

- Misinformation – something untrue which spreads unwittingly

- Disinformation – This transmits intentionally with malicious interest.

These above categories are found by Ontotext which is also used by Pheme.

It is also advantaged by identifying malicious information with the analysis of history and semantics. Hence it search the sources like news outlines, individual journalist, automated bots etc that deny the information and plot evolvement of conversation on social media; network to assess whether it is diffuse with lies.

4. Architecture

The project is based on the WebLyzard and the complete architecture is divided into three layers -- front end, back end and the API as shown in Fig 2. The front end is the client browser where the data are fetched from the back end via websocket or HTTP requests. The

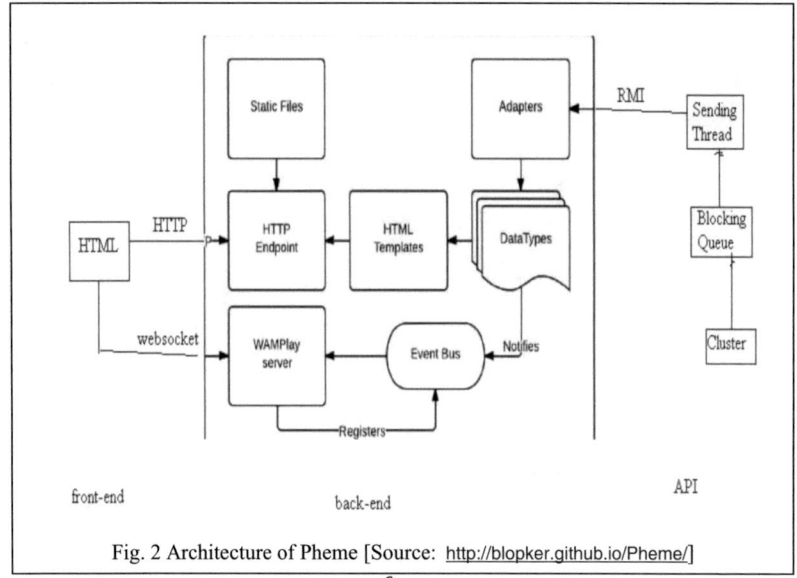

Fig. 2 Architecture of Pheme [Source: http://blopker.github.io/Pheme/]

6

complete interface is signaled with the bootstrap CSS framework where the JQuery creates and manages the websockets. With these it also make compatible for the mobile devices to report the correct viewtags.The back end separates the different components following the model view controller (MVC) design. When the pheme starts, template engine delivers HTML page with the compiled template. Each of these template get the log websocket server URL dynamically which access the database. And when the model updates the complete function is exported to SQL database. Here the new SQL directive enters into database will alert the controllers. For instance, the HTTP controller decides the view to be sent for the browser. Since MVC creates the list of events and whenever a new event occurs, the adapters which are always listening the communication layer convert the newly entered data into the model and register the object event using the RMI communication.But this architecture cannot be with-stand the continue logs so for such contiguous data a non blocking API is added which spawns its thread to buffering and sending the data even in connection lost. The API is designed in a jar file with the consideration of dependencies outside the java so that it can be easily deployed with the existing applications.

5. Exploring Detection

The project apps can be run on mobiles as well as on computers. Since it is a portable so the pheme can be executed from apps or simply through browser. Here for the sake of simplicity twitter is used for demonstration purpose. The word or the query is to be put for testing which would respond with complete graph and keywords on the internet to detect information as seen in Fig. 3.

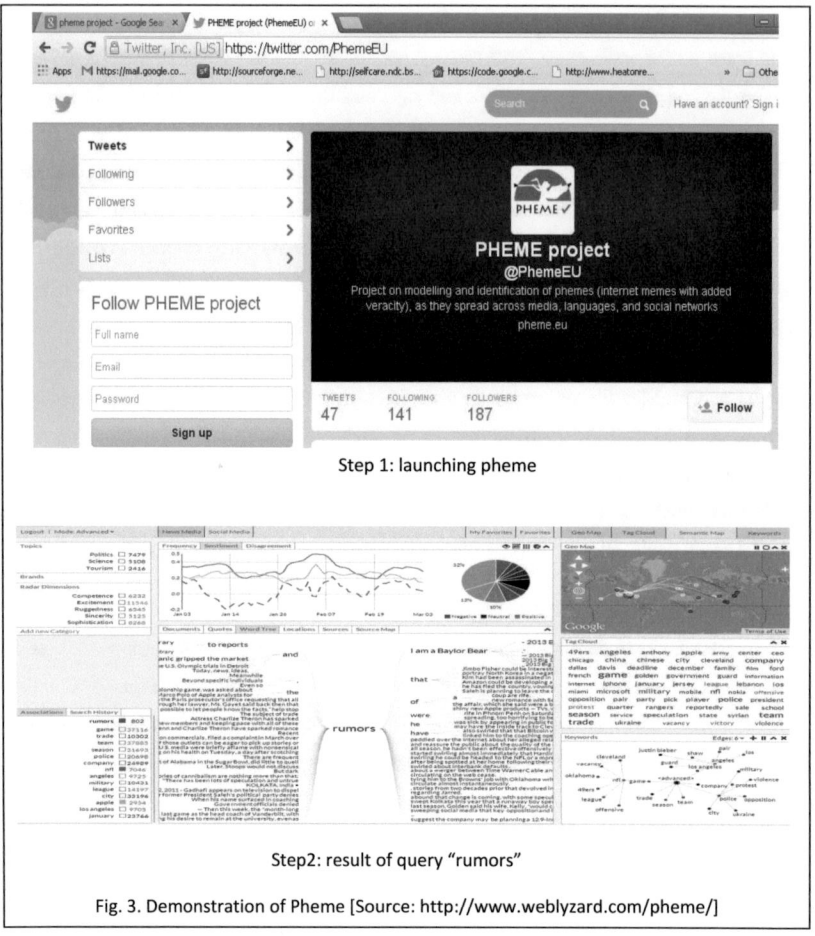

Step 1: launching pheme

Step2: result of query "rumors"

Fig. 3. Demonstration of Pheme [Source: http://www.weblyzard.com/pheme/]

6. Conclusion

The running project will allow the government agencies, emergency services and friends to respond more efficiently to the posts and can be safe ourselves by being the part of such untrue or the lie unknowingly. Pheme's architecture will allow it to grow. Future enhancements will communicate through the event bus. The adapter system allows for flexibility with different APIs. Also, the front end has room to evolve into its own miniature application. The project is still in research which tentatively be furnished by 2016.

7. References

[1] http://charlesmunger.github.com/jpregel-aws/

[2] Grzegorz Malewicz, Matthew H. Austern, Aart J.C Bik, James C. Dehnert, Ilan Horn, Naty Leiser, and Grzegorz Czajkowski. 2010. Pregel: a system for large-scale graph processing. *In Proceedings of the 2010 ACM SIGMOD International Conference on Management of data* (SIGMOD '10). ACM, New York, NY, USA, 135-146.
DOI=10.1145/1807167.1807184 http://doi.acm.org/10.1145/1807167.1807184

[2]Arno Scharl, Albert Weichselbraun and Wei Liu, Tracking and Modeling Information Diffusion across Interactive Online Media, *Int. J. Metadata, Semantics and Ontologies, Vol. 2, No. 3, 2007*

[3] http://www.ontotext.com/sites/default/files/FactForge20-EDF_0.pdf

[4] http://www.ontotext.com/owlim

[5] A real-time user interface for distributed systems. https://github.com/blopker/Pheme/wiki

[6] Martin Soorjoo, The black book of Lie Detection Effective techniques from a Professional Lie Detector, 2009